Greater Than a Tou
The Garden Route
Western Cape Province
South Africa

50 Travel Tips from a Local

Li-Anne McGregor van Aardt

Li-Anne McGregor van Aardt

Copyright © 2017 CZYK Publishing
All Rights Reserved. No part of this publication may be reproduced, including scanning and photocopying, or distributed in any form or by any means, electronic or mechanical, or stored in a database or retrieval system without prior written permission from the publisher.

Disclaimer: The publisher has put forth an effort in preparing and arranging this book. The information provided herein by the author is provided "as is". Use this information at your own risk. Consult your doctor before engaging in any medical activities. The publisher and author disclaim any liabilities for any loss of profit or commercial or personal damages resulting from the information contained in this book.

Order Information: To order this title please email lbrenenc@gmail.com or visit GreaterThanATourist.com. A bulk discount can be provided.

Cover Template Creator: Lisa Rusczyk Ed. D. using Canva.
Cover Creator: Lisa Rusczyk Ed. D.
Image: https://pixabay.com/en/south-africa-garden-route-river-1001433/

CZYK
PUBLISHING

Lock Haven, PA
All rights reserved.
ISBN: 9781522063421

>TOURIST
50 TRAVEL TIPS FROM A LOCAL

Li-Anne McGregor van Aardt

BOOK DESCRIPTION

Are you excited about planning your next trip?

Do you want to try something new?

Would you like some guidance from a local?

If you answered yes to any of these questions, then this Greater Than a Tourist book is for you.

Greater Than A Tourist - The Garden Route, South Africa by Li-Anne McGregor van Aardt offers the inside scope on The Garden Route, situated in the Western Cape Province of South Africa.Most travel books tell you how to sightsee. Although there's nothing wrong with that, as a part of the Greater than a Tourist series, this book will give you tips from someone who lives at your next travel destination. In these pages, you'll discover local advice that will help you throughout your trip. Travel like a local. Slow down and get to know the people and the culture of a place. By the time you finish this book, you will be eager and prepared to travel

Li-Anne McGregor van Aardt

to your next destination.

TABLE OF CONTENTS

BOOK DESCRIPTION

TABLE OF CONTENTS

DEDICATION

ABOUT THE AUTHOR

FROM THE PUBLISHER

WELCOME TO > TOURIST

INTRODUCTION

1. Go Waterfall Hiking
2. Traipse The Tsitsikamma Suspension Bridge
3. Canoe In The Wilderness
4. Jump Off The Bloukrans Bridge
5. Frolic Amongst Proteas In TsitsiKamma
6. Sand-board Down The Highest Dune In South Africa
7. Zip-line Down South Africa's Oldest Zip-line
8. Set Up A Segway Tour Of The Garden Route
9. Stop By Cocomo's In The Wilderness
10. Taste Local Cuisine At Kaai 4 Braai

11. Go Country Style At Crossways Country Kitchen

12. Explore The Knysna Heads' Vistas

13. Talk With The Elephants At The Knysna Elephant Sanctuary

14. Discover The Fynbos Kingdom And House Of Aloes

15. Safari The Addo Game Park Way

16. Ride A Tractor At Featherbed Nature Reserve

17. Swoop Into A Great Day Of Bird Watching

18. Dive Right Into An Ocean Safari

19. Glide Into The Treetops Of Tsitsikamma Forest

20. Take Up A Tour Of The Cango Caves

21. Howl Into A Day At The Wolf Sanctuary

22. Slide On Over To Adventureland

23. Saddle Up To Enjoy The Hog Hollows Horse Trails

24. Kayak Through Tsitsikamma National Park

25. Go Bundu-Bashing At Duiwelsberg 4x4 Trails

26. Pack A Picnic And Explore Woodville Picnic Site

27. Discover The Point Of Human Origins

28. Browse The Great Brak River Museum

29. Have A Whale Of A Time Whale Watching

30. Scope The Local Ware At Plett Market On Main

31. Find Your Fine Art Finesse At Lookout Art Gallery

32. Feel The Sand Between Your Feet At Myoli Beach

33. Tube Into Adventures With Blackwater Tubing

34. Visit Yesteryear With An Historic Walk

35. Reel In Good Times With Plett Fishing Charters

36. Treat Yourself To A Tasty Cuisine At E'Lapa

37. Surf's Up When You Are In Still Bay

38. While Away The Day At The Tin House

39. Dance To Your Own Beat

40. Take A Selfie At The Big Tree

41. Go Green At Outeniqua Farmer's Market

42. Get Decadent With The Oyster Farm Tour

43. Buckle Up And Explore Sedgefield Classic Cars

44. Monkey About At Monkeyland

45. Ascend The Steep Traverse To Sparrebosch Beach

46. Flex Your Mental Muscles At Plett Puzzle Park

47. Peddle A Go-Cart At Redberry Farm

48. Get Lost In The Redberry Maze

49. Explore South Africa's Longest Wine Route

50. Meander By Moonlight In Sedgefield

Li-Anne McGregor van Aardt

Top Reasons to Book This Trip

Our Story

Notes

DEDICATION

This book is dedicated to my family:

To my daughter, Raidin Kairi: thank you for all the lessons you have taught me, and continue to teach us. Continue to travel eternity – we will meet you there.

To my daughters, Aila Arora and Kiyon Kadence: may you always be curious, courageous and travel the path of love supreme; always remember that 'those who wander are not always lost'.

To my pillar - my wonderful, supportive husband, Chase - thank you for being my mirrored soul.

Li-Anne McGregor van Aardt

ABOUT THE AUTHOR

Li-Anne is a wife, mother, musician, writer, and daughter of the Most High. The beauty of everyday life, and the varying ways in which they are displayed in different regions, different cultures, and different demographics ever captivate her. Given the fact that Li-Anne lives in the Western Cape of South Africa, means there is ample opportunity for Li-Anne to explore all the diversities if this wonderful Rainbow Nation.

With her love for all things prose, all things adventure, all things that intrigue, and being able to find joy in the ability to paint a vivid image with just words, combined with Li-Anne's unquenchable wanderlust, it is little wonder why the next logical step would be a written journey into one of Li-Anne's favourite places in her birth country: The Garden Route of South Africa.

Li-Anne McGregor van Aardt

HOW TO USE THIS BOOK

The Greater Than a Tourist book series was written by someone who has lived in an area for over three months. The goal of this book is to help travelers either dream or experience different locations by providing opinions from a local. The author has made suggestions based on their own experiences. Please do your own research before traveling to the area in case the suggested places are unavailable.

Li-Anne McGregor van Aardt

FROM THE PUBLISHER

Traveling can be one of the most important parts of a person's life. The anticipation and memories that you have are some of the best. As a publisher of the Greater Than a Tourist book series, as well as the popular 50 Things to Know book series, we strive to help you learn about new places, spark your imagination, and inspire you. Wherever you are and whatever you do I wish you safe, fun, and inspiring travel.

Lisa Rusczyk Ed. D.

CZYK Publishing

Li-Anne McGregor van Aardt

WELCOME TO > TOURIST

Li-Anne McGregor van Aardt

INTRODUCTION

Stretching out over the expanse of rugged coastlines, lush forestation, treacherous mountain landscapes, and an all-encompassing natural beauty surrounds, you'll be forgiven if you thought you tripped and landed yourself in either Lothlórien or Rivendell, in Middle Earth, from *'The Lord of The Rings' saga. Comprising of a stretch of Southern African land that is so rich in diversity of vegetation, the most unique and extensive of them all being the indigenous to South Africa, and rife in The Garden Route: namely, fynbos. It is with this fact that one ceases to wonder why this region got its name as The Garden Route. Ranging from Mossel Bay, in the Western Cape Province until the Storm's River, in the Eastern Cape, The Garden Route passes through Mossel Bay, Little Brak River, George, Nature's Valley, Knysna and Plettenberg Bay – to name just a few.

Indeed, so majestically immaculate is The Garden Route's vistas, natural fauna and flora kingdom, and welcoming community that you could just as well be traversing a land that fantasies are made of - filled with mystery, adventure, discovery and plain old fun.

* Fun fact: Did you know that the author of this epic saga, J.R Tolkien was actually born in South Africa? (True story)

1. Go Waterfall Hiking

The Garden Route is a great pace to get your hiking boots a-walking, because, let's face it – that's what those boots were made for – walking – and that's just what they'll do. That, and hiking, trekking, mountaineering, trotting, climbing and more..

With over 57 well-known hiking trails to choose from, situated in and around The Garden Route, you would be completely right if you thought that The Garden Route is spoilt for choice, in this department.

Do yourself a favour and try out at least one of the hiking trails that are there for public enjoyment.

For the adventurer looking to take up the famous singing group, TLC, and wanting to go 'chasing waterfalls', there is the Tierkop Trail, situated in Witfontein, George. Here you'll find pine plantations, fynbos, indigenous trees, and an oh-so inviting waterfall.

2. Traipse The Tsitsikamma Suspension Bridge

Perhaps one of the most popular attractions to the Tsitsikamma National Park is the Suspension Bridge. Due to the fact that this bridge spans a distance of 77 metres, and is suspended a mere 7 metres above the rapid flowing Storm's River, does not deter visitors from clambering to experience the vast and pristine vistas of the scenic background.

The Tsitsikamma National Park includes many hiking trails, but this path leading up to the suspension bridge, spans 900 metres and is all encompassing of the immaculate views, and forest terrain you'll need to traverse to get to the bridge.

Built in 1969, the original bridge had to be rebuilt to ensure safety and stability at all times. This project of restoring the bridge was taken up by San-Parks, so we have them to thank for the continual option of being able to experience Tsitsikamma suspended 7 metres up in the air.

3. Canoe In The Wilderness

Find yourself winding down the rapids, having to make split-second decisions, while heading speedily fast down the river terrain towards the white frothy water breaks of the river.

This is very easily done, when you take up the Canoe and Cycle Tour challenge. Being a clear-cut way to enjoying all that The Wilderness has to offer, the Canoe and Cycle Tour is the perfect activity for anyone that fancies him or herself a sporty, outdoor-loving, canoe-careening, cycling fanatic, with energy to burn and an accomplishment to achieve.

As you make your way up the Touw River in your canoe, you may want to keep a close eye out for elusive wildlife, like the Knysna Loerie, as they are so rare to spot – you'd be indebted to Lady Luck if you saw one, indeed.

4. Jump Off The Bloukrans Bridge

Take a leap of faith, a 216 metre leap, off the Bloukrans Bridge, and enjoy the pendulum action of the bungee system, to live another day to tell the harrowing tale of the day you decided to catapult yourself off the 'highest single span arch bridge in the world'.

Bloukrans Bridge is perfect for commercial bungee jumping, as it also consist of a platform, which is used as a launch platform for bungee jumpers, to ensure the pendulum system put in place does as it should, delivers a smooth ride for the bungee jumper.

Also known as the 'highest commercially operated Bungee Jump, from a bridge, in the world' means that when you do the (quite frankly) crazy deed of actually bungee jumping this bridge, you'll be able to add having jumped off the highest bungee bridge in the world to your list of accomplishments.

5. Frolic Amongst Proteas In TsitsiKamma

Proteas happen to be the National Flower of South Africa. The allure and the regal look of this flower, has made it a well-sought after and quite precious member of the flora kingdom.

For more information on Proteas, and a chance to see exactly how the process of growing Proteas, caring for them and finally exporting hem is handled and carried out, when you go to Regyne Farm.

For those of you unfamiliar with the name of this farm, it is important to point out here that it is the 'biggest commercial protea farm in the world'.

For a novel experience, that is actually rather informative as well, head on over to Regyne Farm, and see what the fuss is all about. Experience, first-hand, why this Protea flower is so important to South Africans.

6. Sand-board Down The Highest Dune In South Africa

Make your way to the longest sand-boarding dune in South Africa, a 35 km expanse of sand-boarding goodness. Situate in Mossel Bay, this is one adventure activity that the whole family can take part in, and excel in.

Sand-boarding is relatively easy to get a handle on, so it wouldn't take too long to get your adventurous spirit to soaring. As you start to get the hang of the sand-board, you will no doubt be landing great specials, and tricks and turns while sand-boarding, all it takes is a bit of practice. Okay, okay – a lot of practice.

Whether you're out for a grand ol' time, or simply wanting to take up a challenge, either way, you're bound to have a whopping good time overall. You may fall here and there, but it's then when you'll need to just get back up again.

7. Zip-line Down South Africa's Oldest Zip-line

Tsitsikamma, as you may well have picked up by now is rife with activities, tours, vistas and innovative adventures to take part in. It is of course little wonder then that it is here in Tsitsikamma Forest that the first zip-line adventure was initiated.

Being the oldest zip-line in South Africa now, the zip-line adventure you can experience at Tsitsikamma is indeed an adventure you will not want to miss out on when down in The Garden Route.

Consisting of platforms that are built around ancient, giant Outeniqua Yellowwood trees, that can be as old as 700 years, your safety while getting set up to enjoy your zip-lining adventure through the Tsitsikamma Forest is pretty much guaranteed.

You'll be able to see such an expansive and impressive sight, as you careen down the cable, which is situated 30 metres above the forest terrain, high up in the canopy of the immaculate indigenous trees of the Tsitsikamma Forest.

You'll be enthralled by the entire zip-line experience, down in Tsitsikamma Forest. You best believe that.

8. Set Up A Segway Tour Of The Garden Route

Explore the natural surrounds of the Garden route, namely: Wilderness, Tsitsikamma and the Fancourt Golf Estate in George, in a rather novel way.

Why not take yourself and your family out on a Segway Tour of the above-mentioned regions. The best way to experience the region in a one-on-one manner, right in the midst of all that is happening at any given moment.

The Wilderness Tour lasts up to an hour, and includes a 15-minute orientation and practice session, in order for patrons to familiarise themselves with the Segway vehicle.

The Tsitsikamma Segway Tour also includes a 15-minute training session, to ensure all Segway drivers are adept at handling their vehicle, and the terrain ahead. This tour lasts up to 2 hours long.

The Fancourt Segway Tour is also a 1-hour tour and includes the initial 15-minute orientation session. A great way to experience these beautiful regions without having to break too much of a sweat, while still remaining close to the action.

9. Stop By Cocomo's In The Wilderness

Time for some casual dining that is served in a relaxing, lively atmosphere, and caters to every palette. Cocomo, situated in Wilderness is your best bet, when looking for top-notch quality of service and food, without the pretention and highfalutin aspects that tend to come with many fine-dining establishments.

Cocomo's popularity rests in the fact that the customer always comes first, and there is no pretence as to the down-to-earth manner in which customers are dealt with.

So, for a spot of superb eats, fabulous and friendly service, and a super mellow environment to enjoy it in, there is just no reason not to stop by Cocomo's, while in the Garden Route.

10. Taste Local Cuisine At Kaai 4 Braai

Take off your shoes, and go all out, embracing your carnivorous side, because a stop at Kaai 4 Braai means you're all up for all things meat.

Alfresco dining at it's best, with a fully immersive local flavour, to the décor, name of the restaurant and menu selection, makes Kaai 4 Braai a unique and welcome difference to dining, while in the Garden Route.

Situated on the sandy beach of Mossel Bay, you'll love the way you can tuck into the delectable local cuisine, while squishing your toes between the soft, beach sand.

With it's diverse menu selection, that explores and delivers on local cuisine, be sure to give the South African cuisine a try. From the potjiekos, to the vetkoek selection, to the gourmet boerewors, all the way down to the potbrood with biltong offering.

You just can't go wrong when you make Kaai 4 Braai your dinner destination.

"Traveling – it leaves you speechless, then turns you into a storyteller."

– Ibn Battuta

Li-Anne McGregor van Aardt

11. Go Country Style At Crossways Country Kitchen

Get ready for an all out country-infused menu that delivers perfectly scrumptious meals that will leave you yearning for more country-style goodness.

Situated in Thornhill, along the Garden Route, in the Crossways Farm Village, this special restaurant makes for a great place to chill down for a few hours, maxing and relaxing in the sunshine.

Another great thing about Crossways Country Kitchen is the homely food ware on offer, and the fact that this restaurant endeavours to bring the 'earth to plate' concept of eating to it's daily menu.

This, of course, entails taking fresh produce straight from it's source, and bringing it directly to the dining customer's plate.

Have a wonderful time enjoying everything cosy and homely about Crossways Country Kitchen.

12. Explore The Knysna Heads' Vistas

The two tall pillars that overlook the Knysna Lagoon and quiet little seaside tow of Knysna is surely stuff that legends are made of. With the towering loom that each of the Knysna Heads, a vanguard of note is created, that will make any foe tremble at the prospect of being caught beneath the sheer cliff faces, plunged into the depths of the waves crashing below.

Heaving been a safe haven for fishermen in the days of old, these impressive natural monoliths are a welcome retreat for weary seamen, attempting to navigate their sea vessels through the treacherous sea waters of the Indian Ocean.

The Knysna Heads remain a steadfast beacon to all who lay their eyes on their magnificent splendour. The fact their exquisite vantage points allow for unparalleled vistas, this top tip is indeed a must-see.

13. Talk With The Elephants At The Knysna Elephant Sanctuary

Make a day available when you're in the Garden Route to stop by the Knysna Elephant Sanctuary. Being a trailblazer in that this was the first facility in South Africa that was specifically designed to care for and conserve orphaned elephants in Africa.

What sets the Knysna Elephant Sanctuary apart from other Elephant conservation sites and reserves is the Encounters with Elephants programme, where daily walks with the elephants within the sanctuary are available to the public.

The guided walk with the elephants' tour departs from the Sanctuary's reception area, every 30 minutes, so there really is no excuse as to not taking up the full experience when at the Knysna Elephant Sanctuary.

14. Discover The Fynbos Kingdom And House Of Aloes

Given that the Garden Route got its name due to it's expansive and richly diverse flora kingdom, it is almost a must that I make mention of the House of Aloes.

Situated in Albertinia, along the Garden Route, you will experience a rather informative and educational tour of the House of aloes – where every endeavour is made to provide a wholly factual and rewarding, as well as relaxing experience for visitors to the House of Aloes.

Here you will discover all the hidden mysteries of this plant, all it's healing properties, and why it is considered the miracle plant amongst many African cultures.

You'll be able to purchase a seedling to take home with you, as you are taught the many varying attributes that the Aloe plant carries. Soon, you will be able to rightfully be able to spread the good news about Aloes, and it's extensive healing properties.

15. Safari The Addo Game Park Way

A trip to The Garden Route of South Africa would definitely be incomplete if you did not stop by the Addo Elephant National Park. Situated in Port Elizabeth, along the Sunday's River, this is the final point of your journey along the Garden Route.

Having been established in 1931, as an attempt to conserve 11 elephants that were endangered and of the region, the Addo Elephant National Park as expanded to such an extent that it is now home to over 350 elephants. This very fact is a great testament to the power of conservation and the transformative principles that can be implemented to reverse adverse effects on nature.

Nowadays, this nature reserve is not only home to elephants, but you'll be able to spot some Black Rhinos, many varying species of Antelope, the Cape Buffalo (a staggering 280), and the ever-intriguing and rare Dung Beetle.

Nature lovers will surely be pleased with this top tip.

16. Ride A Tractor At Featherbed Nature Reserve

I've added this top tip in, as I think this probably encapsulates the very essence of the Garden Route. The fact that riding a tractor is fun, and oh so enjoyable, coupled with the fact that it is a symbol of the agricultural industry that is rife in the Garden Route, while also alluding to the rich tapestry of the farm life - that is also synonymous with any regions found along the Garden Route.

The fact that this tractor ride is offered at the Featherbed Nature Reserve also improves on this very fun experience, as it is conducted in the pristine environment and immaculate backdrop of the Featherbed Nature Reserve.

Situated on the Western Head of Knysna, Featherbed Nature Reserve is a privately owned reverse, and a national Heritage Site. Due to the fact that utmost care is taken to preserve this pristine reserve, visitations to the Nature Reserve is strictly controlled, and is only accessible by appointment. Book now to avoid disappointment, as the tractor ride is only one activity that you can get into whe at Featherbed Nature Reserve.

17. Swoop Into A Great Day Of Bird Watching

The Birds of Eden sanctuary is a great way to get acquainted with all things avian, while learning all there is to know about the wide selection of bird species found in this sanctuary.

The Birds of Eden Sanctuary is situated in The Crags, in Plettenberg Bay – along the Garden Route. You'll surely be wowed to find out that this very sanctuary is the largest free-flight Avery in the world, and boasts over 3500 birds that have made this Avery their home. Spanning two hectares, this ginormous dome encapsulates a gorge, surrounded by a vast indigenous forest. You'll find a rather unique ruin, as you make your way through the Avery, and will even be given a chance to explore the walk-behind waterfall. Having opened it's doors to the public in December of 2005, this wonderful bird sanctuary has only grown in popularity. Be sure to add this to your list of things to do when in Plettenberg Bay.

18. Dive Right Into An Ocean Safari

Join in on an Ocean Safari, and experience the wildlife in the ocean, unlike you have ever before. With such a vast array of wildlife to learn about on an Ocean Safari, there is almost not enough time in one given day to be able to explore it all.

By it's very definition, a 'safari' is:

> "a journey or expedition, for hunting, exploration, or investigation".

(Reference source: http://www.dictionary.com/browse/safari)

Which in turn means that by taking part in an Ocean Safari, you will be placing yourself in the wonderful position of being able to observe the many varieties of wildlife, while they exist in their very own habitat.

You will have a great time whale watching on the safari, as well as being able to sight some dolphins too. From seals, to sharks to corals, and just so much more, an Ocean Safari is the way to go to open up the world of the sea to you, and give you a better understanding of the wildlife that exist therein.

19. Glide Into The Treetops Of Tsitsikamma Forest

Get the bird's eye view of the Garden Route, as you take to sky in your paraglide, either flying solo (if you are an experience and license holding paraglider, or via a tandem paraglide for all first time flyers and novice adventurers.

You'll find the jump off point located in Sedgefield, which gives a wholly full comprehensive top-level view of all of the wonder that is Wilderness, and Knysna – from this high up, all that matters is the wind all around you, and the tangible feeling of freedom.

Enjoy an opportunity to also take part in the training sessions, where you can even sign up to join the Basic Paragliding License Course. With this license you will be able to pursue this exhilarating sport, and rack up your jumps all over the globe.

Have yourself a great time, flying on top of the world – while being able to see the immaculate Garden Route with a pseudo-eagles' eye.

20. Take Up A Tour Of The Cango Caves

Located 29-kilometres from Oudtshoorn, along the Garden Route, this South African heritage site comprises of a ridge made up of limestone, which runs parallel to the Swartberg Mountain range.

The Cango Caves boast impressive stalagmites that protrude out of the mineral-enriched floored terrain of the caves. You will also be able to check out the phenomenal stalactites, which form immense icicle-shaped formations that hang from the ceilings.

You'll need to call in advance and book your space in one of the guided tours that take off hourly. There is a Heritage Tour to take, where you'll be taken through the caves, and educated about the heritage these caves hold. There is also an Adventure Tour, which takes you into the deep of the caves – giving an all-encompassing way to experience the Cango Caves.

>TOURIST

"Broad, wholesome, charitable views of men and things cannot be acquired by vegetating in one little corner of the earth all of one's lifetime."

– Mark Twain

Li-Anne McGregor van Aardt

21. Howl Into A Day At The Wolf Sanctuary

The Garden Route Wolf Sanctuary is home to Timber Wolves, African Wild Dogs, Black Backed Jackals, and husky dogs too. This awareness centre is one of the first free roaming wolf sanctuaries in South Africa.

When you plan to visit this Canis Lupus (also known as: the wolf), you'll want to take the following into account, in order to plan your trip accordingly. Feeding times for the wolf is at 16h30 during the warmer months (Oct-Mar) and at 17h30 during the colder months (Apr-Sep). Another great feature that you'd want to call in advance to book for, is the interactive tour that kicks of from 11h00 until 15h00, daily, and it is the 'Walking With Wolves' tour. This is where a fully trained and informative guide takes you through the enclosure, for an up close and personal experience with the wolves in the enclosure.

22. Slide On Over To Adventureland

Picture it: it's a hot summer's day, in the blistering African sun, temperatures keep soaring, and you've had it up to here with trying to cool yourself with your holiday accommodation's AC. Yip, that's it – it's time to grab the kids, and splash into a fun-filled, water sliding day at Adventureland.

This tip is one of my favourites, because it has all the makings of summer-doused memories, hat will last a lifetime. Consisting of water slides, a lazy tube river, and ample lawn areas, Adventureland makes slipping and sliding the best fun ever. Grab your sunnies, your beach umbrella, don't forget the sunblock (it is Africa after all, even if it is he Western Cape Province of South Africa) and whatever you do, don't forget your *towel.

*a little tip I picked up from Douglas Adams

23. Saddle Up To Enjoy The Hog Hollows Horse Trails

Tucked in the expansive and exquisite terrain of the Tsitsikamma National Park, Hog Hollows Horse Trails is sure to give you an uninterrupted, unique way t experience the beauty of The Garden Route.

You have many different Horse riding trails to choose from, in fact there are six. From a mellow 1-hour meadow trail, to a full day's ride into the heart of The Crags, there is a trail to cater to every rider's whimsical fantasy.

You'll be pleased to find that along with your nature seeking horse riding trails, there is also a horse and carriage trail, as well as a Wine Tasting Trail, where riders will get to explore 3 different wine farms in the area. A great way to take in all that the Tsitsikamma consist of.

24. Kayak Through Tsitsikamma National Park

Take up your kayak and explore the Tsitsikamma National Park like you would no other way. Here in the confines of your trusty kayak, you will be able to get a first-hand experience of these pristine natural surrounds, as it can only be seen from the vantage point of the river.

Kayaking your way to your destination, you'll be given ample opportunity to spot the diverse birdlife in the Tsitsikamma. Along with this wealth of aviation activity, you'll be met with many different species of birds, so for all you bird-watchers, be sure to keep an eagle eye out for your favourites.

For a calm, serene and tranquil escape onto the waters of the Storm River, kayaking is a good choice for mode of transport. Not only will you be able to travel great distances with the kayak, but you will be able to see a side of Tsitsikamma that can only be seen and admired by fellow kayakers.

25. Go Bundu-Bashing At Duiwelsberg 4x4 Trails

Try your hand at this 30-kilometre 4x4 trail, and prepare to traverse this route for at least 3 hours. Located in George, just down the Montagu Pass, you'll want to only tackle this trail with your 2x4 or 4x4 (preferably) vehicle.

Dating back to 1776, this route used to only be accessed by horseback, or with an ox-wagon – a true testament to the treacherous adversities the voortrekkers (early settlers) in South Africa had to endure.

Travel this 4x4 trail and you'll get to say you've traversed the Original Trade Route; which leads all the way down to Langkloof.

It is advised to give this trail a go in the early morning, as this route is prone to regular mist occurring in the mid afternoon, with the sun positioned right in front of you in the later afternoon, making for obscure visibility on this trail. Hence why mornings are best.

26. Pack A Picnic And Explore Woodville Picnic Site

Here's your check list for things to bring with you, when you're on your way to spending the day in this magical oasis of green, that could easily be mistaken for being Queen Mab's mystical home: fairyland.

Bring your towel, your swimming gear, your picnic basket, some picnic snacks, and your favourite book - and don't forget the picnic blanket to make the whole picnic experience in Woodville Picnic Site, complete.

Situated in Hoekwil, you'll find this serene picnic spot tucked beneath a small forest of trees. With it's ample green-grassed grounds, picnic tables and benches to relax on, Woodville Picnic Site is indeed a great way to get some relaxation done.

27. Discover The Point Of Human Origins

Spend a day with one of the two scientists that made a phenomenal discovery, 17 years ago, in Pinnacle Point Beach, Mossel Bay – in The Garden Route.

Considered to be actual evidence of the fact that Homo sapiens originated from Africa, in fact, South Africa, this great find turned out to be a turning point for Dr. Nilssen and Jonathan Kaplan. Even 17 years later, this area, attracts many intrigued visitors, daily.

Due to the fragility of the site, and the priceless find, visitors to the site need to book to make an appointment, and only 12 visitors are taken to the site at one given time.

A 3-4 hour tour with Dr. Nilssen himself, the Point of Human

Origins Experience is the comprehensive tour, while a 90-minute guided cave tour is also an option.

Definitely a must-see for anyone interested in learning a bit more about ancient civilizations, and the origins of humans.

28. Browse The Great Brak River Museum

The original schoolhouse, which is now home to the Great Brak River Museum was built in 1908, and is a testament to the great legacy South African's forefathers left behind.

I'm not so much referring to the actual building, but more so the artefacts, old photographs and ancient implements on show at the museum.

Not only is the Great Brak River Museum a great place to come to relive and research the way the Great Brak River inhabitants lived back in the day, but it is also a rich resource, in terms of preserving the stories and heritage of the indigenous people of South Africa, namely, the Khoisan and the Khoe.

Set your sights to finding out all about this quaint little village, and the resourceful inhabitants of the land it encumbers.

29. Have A Whale Of A Time Whale Watching

The Garden Route has so many wonderful lookout spots, and chill areas in an around the coastline, that makes for easy and optimal Whale watching.

The fact that Whales are so prominent in Plettenberg Bay, Sedgefield, Mossel Bay, and Wilderness mean that everyone will be able to spot at least one or two whales, doing what they do best – frolicking, splashing, using their blow-holes and jump-diving.

From Byrde's to Orca's to the Humpback whales, you'll be able to spot them easily and readily, when in The Garden Route.

30. Scope The Local Ware At Plett Market On Main

Markets are always fun, novel, bargain bins – and a place that collects the eclectic. What's not to like about markets? When you're down in the Garden Route, you should do yourself a proper favour, and head on over to Plett Market on Main.

There are 7 food stalls to get your hands on, as well as so many differing varieties of goods on offer – you are bound to find a precious trinket, at least. From leather merchandise, to jewellery, to clothing, books – you name it, you'll probably find it there.

Open & days a week, with ample parking, and a covered roofing area, you'd be remiss if you did not check this tip out.

Should you decide to go to the market on a Wednesday or Friday, you'd be in for a great surprise, as these are the musical nights, where you'll be shaking your hips from 6pm until 9pm. You can even bring your own beverages. How rad is that? Make sure you check it out; you can thank me later.

Li-Anne McGregor van Aardt

"Stuff your eyes with wonder, live as if you'd drop dead in ten seconds. See the world. It's more fantastic than any dream made or paid for in factories."

– Ray Bradbury

Li-Anne McGregor van Aardt

31. Find Your Fine Art Finesse At Lookout Art Gallery

This one is for all those discerning art collectors, and novice art collectors alike, as there is surely something you're bound to find at Lookout Art Gallery that will wow.

When searching for that perfect think piece or conversation piece to place into your home, or perhaps a memento to remind you of your Garden Route travels, you're bound to find the perfect piece of art, and at a reasonable price too.

Even if you're not in the market for any new masterpieces, you are welcome to peruse the offerings from Lookout Art Gallery anyway, as admiration of the fine art elements to be found in Lookout Art Gallery is something locals have come to understand is just the way when visitors see the artistic ware available at Lookout.

32. Feel The Sand Between Your Feet At Myoli Beach

Give yourself the greatest gift, while exploring The Garden Route, and squish the soft-as-chocolate-mousse, golden sands of Sedgefield's Myoli Beach.

Here you'll find a range of sporting activities taking place on any given day, as well as beach goers also revelling in some maximum relaxation in the African sun. Be it surfing, kite-surfing, stand-up paddle boarding, diving, wake-boarding and kayaking – just to name a few – you're sure to be able to find your fun on Myoli. Feeling a bit puckish, after some time in the water? Don't stress, there's a welcoming restaurant situated on Myoli Beach, with a beachside bar located just next to the restaurant. Expect only the best day, when you spend it on Myoli.

33. Tube Into Adventures With Blackwater Tubing

Situated in the midst of The Tsitsikamma National Park, this next adventure must-try is indeed a novel way to take in the beauty surrounds of the Tsitsikamma.

Making use of black tubes, this exhilarating activity kicks off at 7am sharp, and is over by approximately noon, dependent on the water and the conditions of the Storm's River. Directly after your black tubing adventure, lunch will be served.

A trip down the Storm's River, on a black tube is really something unique to try out, and is a great way to build fond, lasting memories of your time in The Garden Route.

Carve yourself a little slice of time, and mould it with a great black tubing adventure, down the Storm's River. Epic tale to tell grandkids ensues.

34. Visit Yesteryear With An Historic Walk

Time for some edu-fun with this next tip; an invitation to explore yesteryear with an historic walk through the seaside town of Mossel Bay, also situated along The Garden Route.

You'll start off the walk at the Mossel Bay Tourism Office, as this is where you will be able to pick up a map that has all the landmarks and historical building locations clearly marked, making it easy for you to wander the streets of the Old Quarter of Mossel Bay, to learn all about this fascinating town.

You'll be taken past buildings of old, some of which were built as early as 1830. There is also an opportunity to check out the Cape St Blaize Lighthouse, a structure that was built during this time.

Be sure to keep an eye out for the terrace housing showcased during this walk, as it is a testament of some fine stone masonry.

> TOURIST

35. Reel In Good Times With Plett Fishing Charters

It's time to break out those fishing rods, bring along your tackle and bait; don't forget your fishing boots, your fishing hat, your peanut-butter and jam sandwiches, and of course – your cold beverages.

When you book a trip with Plett Fishing Charters, you'll be able to get your fishing mode on, and not just any old rock fishing, or pier fishing - nope – this is the real deal! Prepare to go deep sea fishing.

Bait it up, get your rid ready, and throw that line into the deep waters, before you now it, you'll have experienced a day on the wide open ocean, doing what you love best – wind in your hair, wave breaks on your face, what could be better? Truly a day of great times is to be had when taking a cruise with Plett Fishing Charters.

36. Treat Yourself To A Tasty Cuisine At E'Lapa

Grab yourself a low-key al fresco dinner at the restaurant, E'Lapa. Being named after the Sotho word for 'traditional homestead', this restaurant clearly lives up to it's name, as it offers patrons a down-to-earth, cosy, relaxing environment to enjoy your meal with.

Specialising in the gourmet braai (aka barbecue) meal, E'Lapa offers patrons a variety of braaied foods, as well as the option of enjoying a hearty Potjie meal too.

For those not familiar with the Potjie, it is a South African way of slow cooking food, in a black pot over some coals and a fire, to serve up the tastiest stew you have ever tasted.

Be sure to give this locally infused restaurant a try whiel in The Garden Route.

37. Surf's Up When You Are In Still Bay

Still Bay, along the Garden Route is a surfer's haven. Surfers from across the globe make the pilgrimage to Still Bay, to get a taste if the waves out there.

Advanced surfers enjoy the rocky spot, known as Morris Point Cape, where the waves are said to more often than not be rife with high-water tunnels, and are unique in that they wash slowly out to shore.

Another choice spot to surf, for the more professional surfers, is the Jongestontain patch of coast. This surf spot is said to be quite rough, so should only be tackled by pro-surfers.

Novice surfers, grommits and newbie surfers should stick to the gentler breaks of Lappiesbaai.

38. While Away The Day At The Tin House

Start your weekend with a few pre-drinks, some choice food to nibble on, and a signature cocktail or two (or three), when you go to The Tin House.

Known as the place to be on Fridays, you'll want to be sure to book a table, and take part in their famous 'Unwind Fridays' events; leave your worries at the door, and enjoy an evening of great food, great company, and a great atmosphere all round.

The Tin House is indeed the perfect place to get some pre-drinks in before the weekend revelry, so be sure to make it date and enjoy what The Tin House is all about.

39. Dance To Your Own Beat

Join in on an interactive African drum circle, and watch as exuberant gumboot dances further carry the pulsating beat to a crescendo of foot tapping, head-bopping, hands-a-clapping kind of rhythm.

You wont know where your sudden drumming prowess came from, when you join in one of these fully interactive drumming circles, as everyone is there to drum their woes away, and welcome in the primal rhythm that just resonates on every level – putting everything back into perspective again.

Not only are these drumming circles great fun, and a great way to meet new people, locals and visitors alike, but it is a great way to release any tension, any worries, any negativity.

As you hit that bongo, djembe or Ashanti drum, you'll very soon be moving to the rhythm of the beat, and realize that life is nothing but sunshine, nothing but sunshine.

Drum roll please…

40. Take A Selfie At The Big Tree

When in Tsitsikamma Forest, you'll want to get your camera ready, and perhaps even break out that trusty selfie stick. You'll be wanting to have your camera ready for immediate snapping and clicking of the device so as to ensure your selfie with the oldest living thing in the forest is crystal clear and spot on.

So what is the oldest living thing in the Tsitsikamma forest? Well, of course it is the more than 1000-year-old tree, otherwise known as The Big Tree.

I admit, the name is not too phenomenal, or catchy – but perhaps it all balances out, as The Big Tree itself is indeed impressive enough. Standing an impressive 36.6 metres high, with a circumference of almost 9 metres, and a canopy birth of 33 metres, it is safe to say that this Yellowwood Outeniqua tree (Podocarpus Falcatus) is completely in a league of its own.

Li-Anne McGregor van Aardt

"Travel and change of place impart new vigor to the mind."

– Seneca

Li-Anne McGregor van Aardt

41. Go Green At Outeniqua Farmer's Market

Bring the whole family along for this one. The Outeniqua Farmer's Market is a great way to spend a day of fun and games. Being a market where fresh produce, hand-made goods, crafts, arts, comedians, singers and entertainers is just par for the course, this is one market that packs a punch. A very hefty, green punch – that is. Focused on bringing only the freshest of food, and produce to the plate, the vendors of the over 80 stalls and craft stations that operate at the farmer's market ensure that only quality produce, quality goods are to be sourced from this market. Consisting of a covered area, means that the Outeniqua Farmer's Market is open throughout the year, regardless the weather. There is also amply parking space, for over 1200 vehicles.

So, there you have it – no excuse no to checkout the market, buy some local produce and get your green on.

42. Get Decadent With The Oyster Farm Tour

Oysters are synonymous with luxury, decadence, opulence and romance. Which make this tip a great addition to this 50 tips list, as it has all the makings of a James Bond movie – minus all the sabotage and espionage of course.In Knysna, you have the opportunity to learn all there is to know about the Knysna Oyster, the Oyster trade, as a business, and to top it all off, you'll get to taste the wares of your day's focal point.

With the Oyster Farm Tour, you'll be shown exactly where the Knysna Oysters can be found, how to hunt for them, and you'll be given an in depth account of exactly how each process during Oyster farming works.

Quite a great way to get to know more about this supposed aphrodisiac

43. Buckle Up And Explore Sedgefield Classic Cars

Get yourself down to Sedgefield and see for yourself how the Sedgefield Classic Cars have created a niche for themselves. By taking the rides of days gone by, refurbishing them, restoring them, and maintaining an immaculate finished result.

Often times one hears the saying that: 'they don't make it like they used to' - this adage can be true indeed for many of these classic beauties, as the sheer style and decadence that exudes from some of these classic ladies, is just something like a phenomenon.

Be sure to stop on by Sedgefield Classic Cars, and who knows – maybe you even strike it really lucky, and get to experience a jolly ride in one of those vintage masterpieces.

44. Monkey About At Monkeyland

Enjoy some time getting to know all about primates when you take the day to explore and experience all there is to do at Monkeyland. Being the fist free-roaming multi primate sanctuary in South Africa, Monkeyland is indeed the epitome of monkeying around.

Comprising of 12 hectares of indigenous forest, combined with 4 hectares of a protected greenbelt, Monkeyland offers each of the Primates a natural environment to live in.

When you make the mission to visit Monkeyland, be sure to stop by Blue Monkey Café, the restaurant situated within the sanctuary. Here you will find plenty tasty morsels to sink your teeth into.

Savour your experience at Monkeyland, and get to know everything there is to know about primates, in their natural habitat.

45. Ascend The Steep Traverse To Sparrebosch Beach

Avid climbers, outdoor adventurers, and just about anyone looking for a wholesome way to spend the day, why not set yourself a goal to check out the idyllic, private beach: Sparrebosch, in Knysna?

The hiking trail that leads you to the beach is beset with water streams that take you to a secluded bay, and a cascading waterfall that gushes during the rainy season.

Once you've made your way beyond all these landmarks along the way, you'll be rightfully super pleased to reach your private beach destination.

There is a steep climb ahead of all hikers attempting this trail, and should therefore only be attempted by able-bodied individuals, to eliminate any possibilities of injuries.

Those who can and do take up the challenge of Sparrebosch Beach are always richly rewarded by the abundance of beauty surround on the beach, and the prolific wildlife to be found in the rock pools.

46. Flex Your Mental Muscles At Plett Puzzle Park

Stretch your mental capacity by way of some 'brain-nastic' fun, when you head on over to Plett Puzzle Park, in The Garden Route. Not only will you be able to get your adventure on by traipsing the forest surrounds, but you will be met with having to make use of your mental muscles just as much as your regular ones. Take a leisurely stroll through the forest puzzle walk, trekking through the forest surrounds, or try your hand at the 3D maze – the first ever life-size maze in South Africa. And don't worry; if the kiddies are not kept wholly entertained with those 2 unique activities, there is also an exciting rope maze for them to get stuck in.

Situated in Oakhill Farm, Plettenberg, this farm has been growing in popularity each year since 1983, as it's owners, Colin and Wilane Mcloud continue to build, research and create a space that facilitates educational learning and ultimate good times.

47. Peddle A Go-Cart At Redberry Farm

Go the extra mile at the Redberry Farm in George; one of the many towns you'll come across during your Garden Route adventure. Boasting a range of super fun activities, the strawberry farm (ten guesses what sparked the name, Redberry? My guess it's the red coloured berry that the farm is synonymous for…) is a solid favourite for many.

From picking (and tasting) the strawberries straight from the vine, to enjoying a little train ride that takes you all around the farm's perimeter, to being able to take a go-cart for a ride, Redberry Farm almost seems too good to be true.

Rally your troops (read as family and friends) and on your marks, get set – go! Race around the go-cart track, and go as fast as your l4egs will peddle, to find yourself a little slice of go-carting fun.

48. Get Lost In The Redberry Maze

Another great adventure to be had at the Strawberry Farm, Redberry, is to be had when you go exploring into the Redberry Maze.

Made up of over 30 000 hedges and close to 1000 hedge rows, this epic maze is sure you give you a god few hours of exploration and entertainment.

Having a blast while trying to find your way through and out of the maze is only art of this eclectic experience; you'll also be able to learn all about the history of the Strawberry Farm, and how it came to be the fun-filled oasis that it is.

Situated in Blanco, George, Redberry Farm is a must-do, because not only will you be able to race your way out of the maze, and peddle a go-cart about, but you will also be able to enjoy the other activities on offer at Redberry.

Enjoy yourself on the pony rides, bumper boats, train rides, pick some strawberries, for an all inclusive, fully comprehensive day of utter fun.

49. Explore South Africa's Longest Wine Route

Route 62 is considered by many to be the longest wine route in South Africa, wait no – that's not right, in fact – the Cape Route 62 is considered to be the longest wine route in the World.

Also known as the R62 provincial route, this route covers a distance of approximately 850km, from Cape Town to Port Elizabeth. Passing through many quaint little towns and village, you'll find the road unravelling to reveal unparalleled vistas from Montagu to Humansdorp.

Consisting of an expanse of wine farms, speciality restaurants, and crafty titbits here and there, this wine route offers first hand glimpses into another world outside of the bustle you'll find in Cape Town.

The immaculate wine lands of Wellington, Tulbagh, Worcester, Robertson and the Klein Karoo are all to be found along your journey down Route 62.

50. Meander By Moonlight In Sedgefield

Calling all you nocturnal travellers; this tip is especially for you. Take a stroll by starlight from Swartvlei Beach to Gerickes Point, with the aid of your torch (flashlight) and a trusty guide.

As you meander down the beach towards the rock pools and onto Gerickes Point, your trusty, and wholly informative tour guide will alert you to the various nocturnal creatures and wildlife that come awake at night.

This adventure into the night is also a great way for the whole family to take part in a unique activity that not only gets the blood flowing, but also flexes those information-grabbing receptors, as there is a wealth of educational aspects to this Starry Stroll. You'll thank your lucky stars that you heard about this activity, as an experience like this is not easy to come by, making it all the more special and memorable.

Li-Anne McGregor van Aardt

Top Reasons to Book This Trip

- **Natural Surrounds**: From the beaches, to the forests, the hiking trails, horse-riding trails, mountain trails and waterways, The Garden Route is synonymous with immaculate beauty and boasts accessible ways for everyone to experience this relatively untouched oasis of wildlife and an abundance of fauna and flora to boot.

- **Food**: You can be sure to have your taste buds tantalized by the various cuisines on offer through the expansive kilometres that make up The Garden Route. Be it fine wining and dining, classic bistro meals, simple old fast food, or even just a cosy old pub, you're sure to find just the right setting to enjoying the tasty morsels that this adventure will serve up for you.

- **Rainbow Nation**: South Africa is rich with a colourful tapestry of cultures, traditions and it's people do indeed display this great amalgamation of heritages. Ubuntu is an indigenous word, which refers to the concept of community, togetherness, and striving for common goals, while respecting common threads that bind us all. Exploring this great country, getting to know this Rainbow Nation will no doubt be the highlight of your trip to South Africa.

> TOURIST

GREATER THAN A TOURIST

Visit GreaterThanATourist.com
http://GreaterThanATourist.com

Sign up for the Greater Than a Tourist Newsletter
http://eepurl.com/cxspyf

Follow us on Facebook:
https://www.facebook.com/GreaterThanATourist

Follow us on Pinterest:
http://pinterest.com/GreaterThanATourist

Follow us on Instagram:
http://Instagram.com/GreaterThanATourist

Li-Anne McGregor van Aardt

> TOURIST

GREATER THAN A TOURIST

Please leave your honest review of this book on Amazon and Goodreads. Thank you.

We appreciate your positive and negative feedback as we try to provide tourist guidance in their next trip from a local.

Our Story

Traveling is a passion of the "Greater than a Tourist" series creator. Lisa studied abroad in college, and for their honeymoon Lisa and her husband toured Europe. During her travels to Malta, an older man tried to give her some advice based on his own experience living on the island since he was a young boy. She was not sure if she should talk to the stranger but was interested in his advice. When traveling to some places she was wary to talk to locals because she was afraid that they weren't being genuine. Through her travels, Lisa learned how much locals had to share with tourists. Lisa created the "Greater Than a Tourist" book series to help connect people with locals. A topic that locals are very passionate about sharing.

Li-Anne McGregor van Aardt

Notes

Printed in Great Britain
by Amazon